BROKEN ENGLISH
SPOKEN PERFECTLY

Stewart Clark

BROKEN ENGLISH
SPOKEN PERFECTLY

ANY PERSONS (EXCEPT PLAYERS) CAUGHT COLLECTING GOLF BALLS ON THIS COURSE WILL BE PROSECUTED AND HAVE THEIR BALLS REMOVED

The ultimate collection

edda uk

Cambridge 2005

Published by edda uk ltd.
Cambridge
© English version, edda uk 2005

Originally Published by Frifant Forlag, Nesodden 2004
© Stewart Clark
Picture credits: Stewart Clark, except p. 59 Kathy Perez, p. 50 Morten
Stokkan, pp. 48 and 54 Arve Torkelsen. Some pictures are
taken from the Internet where they are circulating.
Jacket Design and Illustration: Alexander S Grenfell
Printed in Latvia, by Preses Nams

ISBN 1-904945-07-4

INTRODOCTION

On one level, this book is fun. And why not? We live in a world where war, tsunami havoc and disaster, murder and destruction are the mainstay of everyday life (if you believe the media). So a bit of humour might just brighten things up. On another level, this book illustrates the flip side of being a world language.

The title of this book was not chosen at random – 'broken English' is perhaps the most widely spoken language in the world. This prompts the question of how many people speak one or another variety of English. The British Council estimates that a quarter of the world's population speaks English to some level of competence (http://www.britishcouncil.org/english/engfaqs.htm#how many). This means that the 375 million native speakers of English are a minority. English is no longer an exclusive language used between Thomas, Richard and Harold but is now the lingua franca of over a billion Tomases, Didricks and Ho-Lings. It also has some degree of official status in around 75 countries. As a result, the hundreds of thousands of well-intended notices, signs and menus found around the world in broken English sometimes produce hilarious results.

Broken English Spoken Perfectly can also be used to analyse why successful communication may go wrong. There is enough to keep the hands of English teachers full for years. We have the typo, glorified in this book by the collection of CVs such as 'left job to ruin my family business', 'skilled in proolreading' and many others that are guaranteed not to enhance your employment prospects. Incidentally, the 'introdoction' typo in the headline above was made by a gentleman in Karachi who also wrote in his email that 'he was interested to establish a cardial business relationship' with me.

Another cause of mistakes in English is mixing up words that look alike such as the café that promises to serve its customers 'with hostility', then there are soundalikes such the menu with 'Sweden sour sauce'. We also have numerous examples of the right word, but in the wrong context such as the fire notice in a hotel in Finland that tells guests to 'expose yourself at the window' and the French-Canadian politician who thanked his audience for their hearty applause with the charming words of 'thank you for giving my wife and me the clap'. Then there are the cultural differences between languages with enough false friends and pitfalls to fill many linguistic minefields.

Broken English Spoken Perfectly is not just about knocking the amazing English that can be produced by foreigners. As mentioned, native speakers need a gentle hint or two. We have the laundrette that promises to dispose of its customers and the classified ad. for teaching staff in a local paper 'Must be proper good at grammer and spelling'. The collection also contains an advert for two classroom assistants at Tower Hamlets, London (spelt 'Lonon' according to them) where about one word in five is not in the dictionary. Even a bastion of correct English usage such as the BBC is included in this collection with a news reader's perhaps telling slip of the tongue 'the unorganized conference…er, I'm sorry, the UN organized conference'.

It has taken over 20 years to gather this collection of broken English (and the publishers are interested in receiving further examples). I would like to thank all my colleagues and friends in the UK, Scandinavia and elsewhere who have helped me in this quest. As an incredible source of broken English has been the Internet, the authenticity cannot always be documented. The location of the sign used in the title of this book is supposed to have been seen in a jewellery shop in Mexico City (with a photo), a Mexican city hotel on the Jucatan Peninsula (1000 km to the east), a shop in Bolivia, and even in an antique shop in Montreal. It is a sign that embodies the status of English in 2005 and may well be scattered all over the Americas.

Wherever, whatever and whoever says or writes what, *Broken English Spoken Perfectly* is a book to enjoy that will bring you smiles, chuckles and a few good laughs.

Contents

'Boyfriends eat turbot'

'Boyfriends eat turbot.'
> *Tony Blair and Gerhard Schröder at a fish restaurant*
> *from 'Berliner Zeitung'*

'I thank you for giving my wife and me the clap. I thank you from the heart of my bottom.'
> *French-Canadian politician*

'This is great day for France.'
> *Richard Nixon at Charles de Gaulle's funeral*

'I am in the beginning of my period.'
> *Newly appointed Danish female minister*

'And now the prick over the "i"…'
> *Danish minister of culture introducing Walter*
> *Mondale*

'For seven and a half years I have worked alongside President Reagan. We've had triumphs. Made some mistakes. We've had some sex…uh…setbacks…'
> *George Bush (senior)*

'Ladies and Gentlemen, welcome to this technical mess.'
Scandinavian politician opening an international trade fair

'I should not say this, but this translation into my language is just Greek to me.'
Greek delegate at meeting in Brussels

The chairman called the meeting to order and asked, 'are there any matters to discuss under the table?'
Meeting at the Commission, Brussels

'I am a man who likes to have my balls in the air.'
Scandinavian businessman

'Pastor's Ass.'
Assistant in the seamen's mission, Pireus, Greece

'Dear friends, we are the same guys as before although we have lost our pricks.'
When Götabanken became Gota bank

'You can have him now.'
Secretary transferring a call

'May I have your office telephone number and your privates?'
Japanese secretary to American businessman

'Owing to a transcription error, an article … on Irish premier Charles Haughley mistakenly read "A man of extreme rudeness". This was intended to read "a man of extreme shrewdness".'
Independent

'Our editors are colleged and write like the Kipling and the Dickens.'
Newspaper, Madras, India

'Bet us your letter of business translation do. Every people in our staffing know English like the hand of their back. Up to the minuet wise-street phrases, don't you know, old boy.'
Advert in Moscow Times

'Our royal guest today is Kong Olav of Norway. Ladies and gentlemen, King Kong Olav.'
Introduction by US senator

'We would like to welcome Mrs M. Thatcher and her husband Mr Pennis Thatcher.'
Newspaper, Spain

The unorganized conference... er, I'm sorry, the UN organized conference.'
BBC Radio

'We are now going over to our reporter who accompanied the teachers' march on one leg.'
BBC Radio

'Be with us again next Saturday at 10 p.m. for "High Fidelity", designed to help music lovers increase their reproduction.'
French radio station

'We hope you have enjoyed our nocturnal emissions and will be with us tomorrow for more.'
French radio station

'I'm a rabid typist'

Quotes from CVs and covering letters

- Curses in liberal arts, curses in computer science, curses in accounting

- Proven ability to track down and correct erors.

- Develop and recommend an annual operating expense fudget.

- Am a perfectionist and rarely if if ever forget details

- Served as assistant sore manager

- Special Skills: "Thyping"

- Left job to ruin my family business.

- Thank you for your consideration. Hope to hear from you shorty

- Education: College, August 1880-May 1984.

15

- I am skilled in proolreading

- Enclosed is a ruff draft of my resume.

- I have an obsession for detail. I like to make sure that I cross my i's and dot my t's.

- Frocklift operator in a warehouse.

- I have lurnt Word and spreadsheat progroms.

- I am sicking and entry-level position.

- I have a doctorate in unclear physics.

BE

Spoken perfectly

'Special Skills: Speak English'

More quotes from CVs and covering letters

- Extensive experiences in Biology

- December 1998: Fired as general director of ...

- Strengths: Ability to meet deadlines while maintaining composer.

- Accomplishments: Oversight of entire department.

- Work Experience: Dealing with customers' conflicts that arouse.

- Suspected to graduate early next year

- My intensity and focus are at inordinately high levels, and my ability to complete projects on time is unspeakable.

- I speak English floatingly

Advert for book on management

- I am experienced in private relations.

- Failed bar exam with relatively high grades.

- Reason for leaving last job: Maturity leave.

- Received a plague for Salesperson of the Year.

- Here are my qualifications for you to overlook.

- You will want me to be Head Honcho in no time.

- Work experience: 25 years in the world of affairs

Spoken perfectly

'You need to have GCSE at leval A-C in Eglish...'

'The tutors also complain of the many sixth-form candidates who appear at interviews in open-neck shirts and whose aplications fomrs abound in spelling mistake.'
Daily Telegraph

'Studding in Cape Town is a great opportunity for me to look at the world from a different angle.'
Student application

'You need to have GCSE at leval A-C in Eglish and Mathematics.'
Advert for primary school teacher, from the Daily Mail

'The Mayor visited the school with his bitter half.'
Local paper, England

'If you think you've got a problem, you should see the head'
School staff-room notice board

'Are you finished? No, I'm Swedish.'
Learn English tape, Finland

'Correctly English in 100 days.'
Book title

'Introducing the Spell-Rite III
Electronic Dicitionary.'
Advert

'Appointment of first headmaster. The Inglish School.'
Advert, Malaga, Spain

'The report was signed by five faulty members of the University.'
Local paper, England

'…must be proper good at grammer and spelling.'
Advert local paper, England

'No bicycles passed this point.'
Sign in a Cambridge college

'I tried to screw the ball in the goal'

'I just want to lie down on the coach.'
Tired Swedish female footballer

'Football-mad mother gives birth to son wearing soccer strip.'
BBC Scotland

'I tried to screw the ball in the goal.'
Female footballer to American press

> ANY PERSONS (EXCEPT PLAYERS)
> CAUGHT COLLECTING GOLF BALLS
> ON THIS COURSE WILL BE
> PROSECUTED AND HAVE THEIR
> BALLS REMOVED

'Screw down your expectations. We wanted to play with long balls.'
Danish footballer at press conference

'Skiers must be raped before crossing the pass.'
Sign in Switzerland

'The skier took off with a tremendous fart.'
Norwegian reporter commentating ski jumping

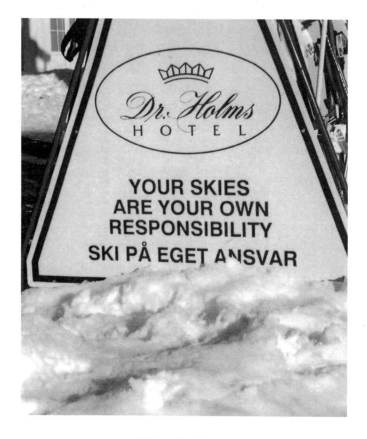

Ski rack, Norway

'Moonshine skiing.'
Student ski festival

"Rugby is a game for men with odd-shaped balls'

'We take your bags and send them in all directions'

'Please feel yourself at home.'
Welcome sign airport, Taiwan

'When passenger of foot heave in sight, tootle the horn. Trumpet him melodiously at first, but if he still obstacles your passage then tootle him with vigor.'
Car rental brochure, Japan

'Press 1 for immediate transport with a common car.'
Taxi company, Norway

'Be in Trouble. Please call 110!'
Public safety sign, China

Sign on Japanese taxi

'…Baroque, judging by the style of panting.'
Cathedral guide to artwork, Prague

Kinki Nippon Tourist Company was the name of Japan's second-largest tourist agency. However, after it kept receiving requests for unusual sex tours, Kinki Nippon changed its name.

'Dai Young Travel.'
Advert, Korean paper

'If the ship sinks walk quickly to the liferafts. Do not swim.'
Notice on Turkish ship

'In case of emergency, the lifeguard are under the seat.'
Ferry, Puerto Rico

'Helpsavering apparata in emergings behold many whistles! Associate the stringing apparata about the bosoms and meet behind. Flee then to the indifferent lifesaving shippen obediencing the instructs of the vessel chef.'
Ship notice, Russia

Tourist brochure, Norway

'In the close village you can buy jolly memorials for when you pass away.'
Tourist brochure

'Don't get into this.'
Road sign on 'do not enter' symbol, Japan

'Stop: drive sideways.'
Detour sign, Japan

'Beware of greasy corner where lurk skid demon. Cease step on, approach slowly, round cautiously, resume step on gradually.'
Road guide, Japan

'Passage of deformed man supermarket.'
Access for disabled people, China

'Any failure to keep an order and infringement of on-board regulations may cause unpredictable " consequences".'
Safety instructions on plane, Russia

'Kindly use the lavatory stationed here on the gallery.'
Sign at Scandinavian airport

'Do not put foreign bodies into the lavatory.'
Airline, Norway

'Bag to be used in case of sickness or to gather remains.'
Spanish airline sick bag

'We take your bags and send them in all directions.'
Airline, Denmark

Host: 'Do you want to use the rest room before we drive cross State?'
Scandinavian au-pair: 'No, I can do it in the car.'

'Excuse me, what's the fart limit?'
Speeding Scandinavian driver to a local bobby

'Give me your love and I will make you peel at home.'
Travel advert, China

'Broken English spoken perfectly'

Hotel facilities

'Mt. Kilimanjaro, the breathtaking backdrop for the Lodge. Swim in the lovely pool while you drink it all in.'
Hotel, Africa

'Choose between a room with a view on the sea or the backside of the country.'
Hotel, Africa

'Hot and cold water running up and down the stairs.'
Hotel, Sweden

'Hua Tian Hotel is among the few best foreign affairs hotels.'
Hotel, China

'If this is your first visit to the USSR, you are welcome to it.'
Hotel, Russia

'This hotel is renowned for its peace and solitude. In fact, crowds from all over the world flock here to enjoy its solitude.'

Hotel, Italy

'Built in 1888 and fully restored in 2000…built to resemble a mid-evil castle.'

Florida hotel

'Rooms for guests with allergy sufferers.'

Hotel, Norway

'In a restructed ancient villa, they works, with 23 comfortable and calm rooms… all equipped of balcony or terrace is enjoyed un'charming sight. The evening is assisted to a wonderful sunset.'

Hotel, Italy

'The provision of a large French widow in every room adds to the visitors comfort.'

Hotel, Spain

'Good appearance please no watermelon please.'

Hotel, China

'Broken English spoken perfectly.'

Hotel, Mexico

'Mousse hunting is our speciality.'

Hotel, Norway

'Suggestive views from every room.'

Hotel brochure, Italy

'Invinsible service is available for your rest not being disturbed.'

Hotel, China

'The manager has personally passed all the water served here.'

Hotel, Mexico

'The tower is profoundly situated in the ground and has the only revolting restaurant in Norway.'

Revolving tower restaurant, Norway

'Guests are requested not to smoke or do other disgusting behaviours in bed.'

'Do not lock the door as we have lost the key.'
Hotel, Ireland

'Please do not bring solicitors into your room.'
Hotel bedroom, Thailand

'Guests are requested not to smoke or do other disgusting behaviours in bed.'
Hotel bedroom, Japan

'Cooles and heates: if you want condition of warm air in your room, please control yourself.'
Hotel air-conditioner, Japan

Dear Guests!
The time will be turned back by one hour,
3 am Sundaymorning due to daylight
saving time so don't forget to change
your watches!

Radisson SAS

'Is forbidden to steal hotel towels please. If you are not person to do such thing is please not to read notis.'
Hotel, Japan

'Non-smoking forbiden.'
Hotel, Jordan

'If set breaks, inform manager. Do not interfere with yourself.'
Hotel TV, Serbia

'It is not allowed to come into the building with feet full with sand.'
Beach hotel, Spain

'Visitors are expected to complain at the office between 9 and 11 daily.'
Hotel, Athens

'Let us know about an unficiency as well as leaking on the service. Our utmost will improve it.'
Hotel, Yugoslavia

'Please leave your values at the front desk.'
Hotel, Paris

'Contact the concierge immediately for informations. Please don't wait last minutes then it would be too late to arrange any inconveniences.'

Hotel, Italy

'(Guests are) not to perambulate the corridors in the hours of repose in the boots of ascension.'

Mountain hotel, Austria

'Because of the impropriety of entertaining guests of the opposite sex in the bedroom, it is suggested that the lobby be used.'

Hotel, Zurich

'The minibar witch is in your room.'

Hotel notice, Norway

'To stop the drip, turn cock to right.'

Hotel bathroom, Finland

'Why not try our sauna baths? If you are lucky you might get a sausage.'

Hotel notice, Finland

'Please to bathe inside the tub.'

Hotel bathroom, Japan

'When you take a bath, please close the door and switch on the fun without fail.'

Hotel bathroom, China

'If you wish disinfection enacted in your presence, cry out for the chambermaid.'

Hotel, Madrid

'The flattening of underwear with pleasure is the job of the chambermaid.'
Hotel, Yugoslavia

'Our maids are especially selected for your service. Do whatever you want with them.'
Hotel, Yugoslavia

'You are invited to take advantage of the chambermaid.'
Hotel, Japan

'Peoples will left the room at midday of tomorrow in place of not which will be more money for hole day.'
Hotel, Madrid

'Guests should announce abandonment of their rooms before 12 o'clock.'
Hotel, Sarajevo

'All rooms not denounced by twelve o'clock will be paid for twicely.'
Hotel, Budapest

'Please hang your order before retiring on your doorknob.'
Hotel, Turkey

'Mad service daily 8-12.'
Hotel, Mexico

'If you wish breakfast, lift the telephone and our waitress will arrive. This will be enough to bring up your food.'
Hotel, Israel

'To call room service, please open the door and call room service.'

Hotel, Turkey

'Breakfast is severed between 5:30 am and 9:00 am.'

Hotel, Vietnam

'Breakfast is served in the 1st floor.'

Hotel, Berlin

'A sports jacket may be worn to dinner, but no trouser.'

Hotel, France

'We wish you sweat dreams.'
Sign on pillow in hotel

'In case of fire...expose yourself at the window'

'All fire extinguishers must be examined at least five days before any fire.'
Hotel, London

'Please to evacuate in hall especially which is accompanied with rude noises.'
Hotel, Turkey

'Dear Guts, In order to prevent possible fire damages we kindly ask you to consider the following rules.'
Hotel, Romania

'In case of fire, please stuff a towel under the door and expose yourself at the window.'
Hotel, Finland

'In case of fire, please read this.'
Hotel, Saudi Arabia

'In case of fire, do your utmost to alarm the hotel porter.'
Hotel, Vienna

'Fire! It is what can doing, we hope. No fear. Not ourselves. Say quickly to all people coming up down everywhere a prayer. Always is a clerk. He is assured of safety by expert men who are in the bar for telephone for the fighters of the fire to come out.'

Hotel, Rome

'In case of emergency, say No.'

By telephone in hotel, Germany

'I will up, I will down'

'Please do not use this lift when it is not working.'
Hotel lift sign, Quatar

'The lift is being fixed for the next day. During that time we regret that you will be unbearable.'
Hotel lift, Bucharest

'To move the cabin, push button for wishing floor. If the cabin should enter more persons, each one should press a number of wishing floor. Driving is then going alphab etically by national order.'
Hotel lift, Belgrade

'Bicycle don't take the staircase.
Don't protrude the tartness and keenness out the staircase.'
Elevator notice, China

'I will up, I will down.'
Hotel lift, Norway

'Do not reverse into lift while lit up.'
Hotel lift, Leipzig

38

'The private beach to be reached by a lift from inside directly, complete the undiscussable peculiarities of this unit.'

Hotel, Italy

'No jumping from the lift. Survivors will be prosecuted.'

Ski lift, Alps

'Erection deck.'

Lift notice, Japan

'Enter the cabin of full lighting only and never backwards.'

Lift sign, Germany

'Special cocktails for the ladies with nuts'

'After one visit we guarantee you will be regular.'
Bar, India

'We serve five o'clock tea at all hours.'
Café, France

'The shadiest cocktail bar in town.'
Bar, Thailand

'When the crowded you get table in another parson.'
Bar, Japan

'We have a room where you can change baby.'
Café, Norway

'Don't stand outside and be miserable. Come inside and be fed up.'
Bar, Japan

'Open seven days a week and weekends.'
Bar, USA

'Members and non-members only.'
Disco, Mexico

'Ladies are requested not to have children in the bar.'
Cocktail lounge, Norway

'Special cocktails for the ladies with nuts.'
Bar, Japan

'Smarts is the most exclusive disco in town. Everyone welcome.'
Disco, England

'With or without a date and in summer – plus open air banging-bar.'
Disco, Spain

'Good clean dancing every night but Sunday.'
Dance hall, USA

'We serve you with hostility'

'We reserve the right to serve refuse to anyone.'
Japan

'Customers who find our waitresses rude ought to see the manager.'
Kenya

'Emergency snakes available at all hours.'
Hotel, Ethiopia

'We serve you with hostility.'
Chinese restaurant

'Come broil yourself at your own table.'
Hong Kong

'As for the tripes serves you at the Hotel Monopol, you will be singing its praise to your children as you lie on your deathbed.'
Poland

'Yes, we are less dirty.'
  Indian restaurant

'You have no reason to try our best restaurant.'
  Indonesian restaurant

'Lunch served you from 12:30 to mid-October.'
  Indonesian restaurant

'Welcome to our French brassiere.'
  French brasserie, Norway

'If you are satisfactory, please tell your friends. If you are not satisfactory, please tell the waiter.'
  Chinese restaurant

"Assaulted artichokes" or "fumigated sausage"?

Starters:

Chess on toast
India

Pooridge painapple
India

The Goo
Japan

Rather burnt land slug
Thailand

Beef broth with ancient
bohemian pasto balls

Czech Repubic

Cheese tomato garlic sand witches
India

Old salt cooked the natural way
France

Children sandwiches

Humans on brown roll
India

Restaurant Radnice

Bill of fare   Kč

Cold hors d´ oeuvres:

120g	Chicken salad with pine-apple	49,-
120g	Cheese variation	49,-
50g	Lobster coctail	59,-
50g	Smoked salmon, butter, lemon	69,-

Soups:

Beef broth with ancient bohemian pasto balls	19,-
Garlic soup with ham and cheese	22,-
Borshch	25,-
Broccoli cream	25,-

Warm hors d´ oeuvres:

50g	Ham-roll with asparagus, fried cheese	49,-
70g	Grilled vegetables in a dish of potatoes	49,-
100g	Seafood salad	69,-
6ks	Snails with herbal butter, toasts	110,-

Grilled fish:

200g	Grilled trout, herbal butter, lemon	119,-
150g	Pickled salmon in provencal oil, lemon	159,-
150g	Halibut on fresh herbs, lemon	159,-
150g	Spiny lobster back with cream sauce, lemon	259,-
150g	Grilled tiger crayfish, lemon	259,-
200g	Fish plate Ocean	199,-

Poultry:

150g	Chicken lockets with sesame seed	119,-
150g	Chicken chest filled with ham and cheese, cheese sauce	119,-
150g	Chicken breast on honey with apples	119,-
150g	Chicken meat in ancient bohemian manner	119,-
150g	Fried chicken steak, lemon	119,-

Game:

150g	Wild board steak on season spice /idle/	189,-
150g	Hart steak on red wine	189,-
150g	Poacher's feast	189,-

Mutton:

150g	Lamb medailons with bacon	139,-
150g	Lamb joint on garlic with cheese	139,-
150g	Mutton spike „Shepherd"	139,-

Czech Republic

Teppan Yaki, before your cooked right eyes
Deep fried fingers of my lady
India

Fried flesh water shrimps
Japan

Caab meet batter rice
Japan

Onion snakes
India

Toes with butter and jam
Bali

Children soup
India

Fried steam
India

Frozen soup with peccadilloes
Patato soup with garbage

Sweden sour sauce
India

Cram chowder
Canada

Egg dishes:

Scrap-heap eggs

Bold egg
India

Eggs with a reindeer
Sweden

46

Benedict that smells like an egg
Israel

Vegetarian dishes:

Pastes and meatless meals
Czech Republic

Fried rice with peppers the way
you lick it

Vegetable staff omelet
India

Salad with the gardener

Salad a firm's own make
Poland

Spawned cabbag

Limpid red beet soup with cheesy dumplings
in the form of a finger
Poland

Assaulted artichokes

Beat roots

Vegitational beef soup
Brazil

Split tummy egg plant

Mess potato
India

Mussed potato
India

Spotted potato
India

Smashed potato
India

**ХАМПОУРГКЕР
HUMBURGER**

Meat dishes:

Grilled lamp ribs
Spain

Chessburger
Poland

Buttered saucepans and fried hormones
Japan

Rissole of Lady's thigh

Beaf casserole with rise
Norway

Beef rashers beaten up in the
country people's fashion
Poland

Arm of gipsy

Pork with fresh garbage
Vietnam

Bowels in spit

Lampent rails

Sloin financier
Indonesian nazi goreng
Hong Kong

48

Broiling of trellis Dreaded veal cutlet
with potatoes in cream
China

Suckling pin

Wild board steak on season spice
Czech Republic

Beef on a spear
Norway

Hot dok
Poland

Guinea-Pig Breast
Slovakia

Jerked meat

Sir Loin steak with potato cheep
Singapore

Chopped cow with a wire through it
Greece

Fumigated sausage

Lioness cutlet
Egypt

Fillet streak and poptoes
Hong Kong

Roat poik Chinese restaurant
USA

Bowels in sauce
Greece

Fowl:

Peking duck with sweat and sour sauce
Norway

Boys style little chickens
Spain

Chicken meat in ancient
bohemian manner
Czech Republic

Chicken to despise

Extract of fowl, peached or sunnyside up
France

Breast of foul chef

Utmost of chicken fried in bother
Macao

Roasted duck let loose
Poland

A half cock of country woman

Half a cock in dragon sauce
France

Turkey meat, salad and sos
Poland

Hen blood stew

Chicken seek kebab
India

Cock in wine
Egypt

Very best meat of chest of duck
cooked for hours in its own grease
France

Fish:

Pasta with voracious clams
Italy

Fish rotty and spaghetti bolograese
Israel

Fried sheath-fish with Fogosh

Miller's wife style

Cod with peas and potato moose
Sweden

Fried fishermen
Japan

French fried ships
Egypt
Shrimp nets

Rape in the Madrid fashion
Spain

51

Boiled Frogfish

Fisherman's crap soup
Greece

Rape, seamanlike style

Friend cod

Goose barnacles
Spain

Pike in Athenians

Muscles of Marine Lobster Thermos
Egypt

Brood of eels

Cold shredded children and sea
blubber in spicy sauce
China

Dessert:

Waffies
Thailand

Tarts of the house
Spain

Roasted jam to the American style

Chocholate mouse
Hong Kong

Tart with rubber chocolate

Strange cheese

Honei limon craps
India

Sweat from the trolley

French creeps
USA

Curled milka sleep

Mixed fruit and whalenuts
Norway

Finest moldy cheese
Japan

Fumigated smocked cheese

Fried milk

Banana pen cake
India

Fried friendship
Nepal

Strawberry crap
Japan

Coffe and snakes
Germany

Ha Ha Fortune cookies
Chinese restaurant, USA

Special today – no ice cream
Switzerland

Please try the tarts of the house.
Available for your delight on the trolley.
Egypt

Snackbar Crete

Wine list:

Red wind / white wind

Our wines leave you nothing to hope for.
Switzerland

Slop brandy

Pain and wine included
Spain

BE

Spoken perfectly

'Dirty Water Punishment Place'

'Please do not feed the animals. If you have any suitable food, give it to the guard on duty.'
Zoo, Hungary

'Children found straying will be taken to the lion house.'
Zoo, Japan

'No smoothen the lion.'
Sign on lion cage, Czech zoo

'Would you like to ride on your own ass?'
Donkey rides, Thailand

'Take one of our horse-driven city tours. We guarantee no miscarriages.'
Tourist agency, Czech Republic

'Happy Holiday Walkings in Micro-Ass.'
Beach sign, Spain

'We will embark for the island of Lobos, where we will have plenty of time to have a swim and admire the marines' bottoms.'
Tourist brochure, Canary Islands

'Boomerang used for killing birds made of wood.'
Museum, Cairo

'The museum is building now – sorry for the visitor.'
Museum, Thailand

'Do not use the diving board when the swimming pool is empty.'
Pool, Sri Lanka

'Swimming forbidden in the absence of a saviour.'
Pool, France

'Foreign guests are requested not to pull cock in tub.'
Public baths, Japan

'Entrance on the backside.'
On front door of an Interrail centre, Norway

'It is forbidden to enter a woman even a foreigner if dressed as a man.'
Temple, Bangkok

'It is strictly forbidden on our black forest camping site that people of different sex, for instance, men and women, live together in one tent unless they are married with each other for this purpose.'
Sign in campsite, Black Forest, Germany

'Do not spit here and there.'
Sign, Calcutta

'Commit No Nuisance.'
Sign, Calcutta

'No boots allowed on the bitch.'
Beach sign, Germany

'Foot wearing prohibited.'
Sign by shrine, Burma

'The grass you must not march on him.'
Park notice, Belgium

'Dirty Water Punishment Place.'
Sewage treatment plant, map Tokyo

'Please waste.'
Trash can sign, Japan

'These seats are reserved for those with relations to the French police.'
Eurostar notice, Chunnel

'Mothers, please wash your hans before eating.'
English sign, German cafe

Japan

'Norway's oldest sweet chestnut. The young leaves have a hairy backside.'
Arboretum, Balestrand, Norway

'No automobiles. Pederasts only.'
Car park sign, Spain

Temple notice, India

'Our toilets are closed, in the meantime use platform 6'

'Don't miss the garden party. Bring an umbrella. No toilet facilities provided.'
Advert, local paper, England

'Toilets may be used only once during running of the train.'
Train notice , Finland

'Our toilets are closed, in the meantime use platform 6.'
British Rail

'The Town Hall is closed until opening. It will remain closed after being opened. Open tomorrow.'
Town Hall, England

'Quicksand. Any person passing this point will be drowned. By order of the district council.'
Somewhere in England

King's College, Cambridge

'Mental Health Prevention Center.'
> *USA*

'Terminal Drugs'
> *Bus terminal, USA*

'We will sell gasoline to anyone in a glass container.'
> *Petrol station, USA*

'Please do not smoke near our petrol pumps. Your life may not be worth much but our petrol is.'
> *Petrol station, England*

'Parking for birds only.'
> *Parking area, Massachusetts*

'The crane will attack your vehicle.'
> *Dock sign, Spain*

'If this sign is under water, the road is impassable.'
> *Road sign, USA*

'Drive carefully: Auto accidents kill most people from 15 to 19.'
> *Highway, USA*

Road sign

'Elephants please stay in your car'
   Safari park

'Slow cattle crossing. No overtaking for the next 100 yrs.'
   Sussex road, England

'My father say's condom's don't work.'
   Bumper sticker

'Recruitment at it's Best!'
   Army recruitment office

'In case of fire, evacuate the building. Do not use stairways. Do not use elevators.'
   Bank, Boston

'Would the person who took the step ladder yesterday please bring it back or further steps will be taken.'
Office, England

'After tea break staff should empty the teapot and stand upside down on the draining board.'
Office, England

'Braille instructions please see below.'
Office building, Denver

'Nurses are required to wear nothing but white hose.'
Hospital, USA

Pub, England

'Bell out of use, please use knockers.'
Outside club

'Visitors with reading difficulties should proceed to front desk for information.'
Community centre, England

'Night watchman patrols this area 24 hours a day.'
Building site

63

'Waitresses required for breakfast.'
Café advert

'Closing down, thanks to all our customers.'
Outside factory

'Tenants not paid by the 15th of the month will be terminated.'
Garage, USA

'Guard dogs operating.'
District Hospital

'Veterinarian/Taxidermist. Either way, you get your dog back.'
Vet's office

'The farmer allows walkers to cross the field for free, but the bull charges.'
Notice in a field, England

'Persons are prohibited from picking flowers from any but their own graves.'
Cemetery

'Due to increasing problems with litter louts and vandals we must ask anyone with relatives buried in the graveyard to do their best to keep them in order.'
Circular from a parish in Wiltshire

'Lay for the ride at the ticket office. Children over 1.20 metres must lay more.'
Notice by Great Wall of China

'We have the wind'

'Gentlemen's throats cut with very sharp razors with great care and skill. No irritating feeling afterwards.'
Barber's shop, India

'English well talking here speeching American.'
Shop sign, Majorca

'Closed between Merry Christmas and a Happy New Year.'
Grocery shop, Oslo

'Dickfish.'
Fish shop, Brussels

'Tarte Julie.'
Art gallery, Brussels

'We have the wind.'
Sign in supermarket with fan, Bali

'Time to re-tire.'
Tyre store

'First class loafer.'
Baker's shop, Kashmir

'Please don't handle the fruit. Ask for Debbie.'
Greengrocer's shop

'Closed due to illness.'
Health food shop

'Out to lunch: if not back by five, out for dinner also.'
Outside photographer's studio

'Ask about our plans for owning your home.'
Advert from loan company

'A. Virgin & Son.'
Shop sign, London

'No appointment necessary. We'll hear you coming.'
Exhausts and mufflers

'Ears pierced while you wait. Pay for two and get another one pierced free.'
Beauty parlour

'Haircuts half price today. Only one per customer.'
Barber's shop, Beijing

'Big pre-Christmas sale. Come in and mangle with the crowd.'
Department store

'Bargain basement upstairs.'
Department store, London

'We dispense with accuracy.'
Chemist, England

'Shoplifters will be beaten over the head with an organic carrot.'
Health food shop

'If you feel we have failed you in any way we shall be only too pleased to do it again at no extra charge.'
Dry-cleaners

'We do not tear your clothing with machinery. We do it carefully by hand.'
Dry-cleaners

'Anyone leaving their garments here for more than 30 days will be disposed of.'
Dry cleaner's, England

'Automatic washing machines: Please remove all your clothes when the light goes out.'
Laundromat

'We stand behind every bed we sell.'
Furniture shop

'No children allowed.'
Maternity ward notice

'Go away!'
Travel agent, Spain

'Ladies, leave your clothes here and spend the afternoon having a good time.'
Laundry, Rome

'Come inside and have a fit.'
Clothing store, Brussels

'Fur coats made for ladies from their own skin.'
Sign in a Swedish furrier's

'Drop your trousers here for best results.'
Sign in a Bangkok dry cleaner's

'Men's Briefs. Try them! They're Comfartable.'
Menswear store, Taiwan

'Order your summers suit. Because is big rush we will execute customers in strict rotation.'
Sign in tailor's shop, Rhodes

'Ladies may have a fit upstairs.'
Sign outside tailor's shop, Hong Kong

'Dresses for street walking.'
Outside dress shop, Paris

'Caution: Avoid dropping air conditioners out of windows'

'Instruction inside the box:
To avoid condensation forming, allow the boxes to
Warm up to room temperature before opening.'
    US guide to setting up a new computer

'On startup: No keyboard detected. Press any key to
continue.'
    Error message 1, on PC

'Keyboard not detected. Press F1 to continue.'
    Error message 2, on PC

'Do not attempt to stick head inside deck, which may
result in injury.'
    Japanese GameCube instruction manual

'Do not allow children to play in the dishwasher.'
    Instruction manual

'Warning! This program should not be used in flight training! Death or serious injury could result!'
Microsoft Flight Simulator 2000

'Do not spray into electrical outlet.'
On a hose nozzle

'Warning: Do not use while sleeping.'
Hair dryer

'Warning: Do not use while taking a shower.'
Hairdryer

'Do not activate with wet hands.'
Automatic hand dryer

'Not to be used for anything else.'
Food processor, Japan

'Caution: Avoid dropping air conditioners out of windows.'
Air conditioner

'Do not use to pick up gasoline or flammable liquids. Do not use to pick up anything that is currently burning.'
Vacuum cleaner

'Warning: Never iron clothes on the body.'
Clothes iron

'Do Not Insert Curling Iron Into Any Bodily Orifice.'
Curling iron

'Not for use as an aquarium.'
On a blender

'For indoor or outdoor use only.'
   Chinese-made Christmas lights

'For indoor use only.'
   Outdoor icicle lights

'This floodlight is capable of illuminating large areas, even in the dark.'
   Floodlight

'To put a call on Hold: Press "Hold".'
   Telephone instruction book

'Be kind - rewind.'
   Rental DVD

'Best when used with MiniDisc recorders and players.'
   Minidisc player

'Toaster: A gift that every member of the family appreciates. Automatically burns toast.'

'Not Dishwasher Safe.'
TV remote control

'This camera will only work when film is inside.'
Camera instructions

BE

Spoken perfectly

'Warning: Tarts may be hot'

'Contents under pressure. Cap may blow off.'
> *Bottle of coke*

'Do not put boiling water or more than 10% alcohol in this cup.'
> *Glass cup*

'Open other end.'
> *On the bottom of coke bottles*

'Suitable for vegetarians.'
> *Mineral water*

'Warning: Remove label before placing in microwave.'
> *Champagne*

'Consumption of alcoholic beverages impairs your ability to drive a car or operate machinery, and may cause health problems.'
> *Beer*

'Warning - Contents may be hot.'
> *McDonald's coffee*

'Do not peel label off.'
On the back of a drink bottle label

On the bottom: "Keep Upright".
Fruit juice carton

'After opening, keep upright.'
On bottle-top of milk drink

'Shake well and buy often.'
Soy milk

'Caution: Will be hot after heating.'
Pudding

'Warning: Tarts may be hot.'
Toaster Tarts

'Serving suggestion: defrost.'
Frozen dinner

'Caution: Ice cream is cold.'
Ice cream

'Artificially Flavored Real Fruit.'
Bakery cherries

'Ingredients: Carrots.'
Farm carrots

'Warning: High in sodium.'
Container, salt

'Warning: This product contains nuts.'
   Packet of peanuts

'Warning: May contain traces of nuts.'
   Almond Bar

'Instructions: open packet, eat nuts.'
   Peanut pack, airline

'Peel fruit from cellophane backing before eating.'

'Do not eat packet.'
   Pepperoni pizza

'Instructions: For proper food safety and quality, use the following directions: Do not eat pizza without cooking.'
   Cheese pizza

'Do not turn upside down!'
   On bottom of pizza packaging

'Warning: While cooking be sure to place crust side down.'
   Pizza

'Take the pizza out of the plastic, then heat it.'
   Pizza

'For best results, remove cap.'
   Cheese snacks

'You could be a winner! No purchase necessary. Details inside.'
   Crisps

'Directions: Drip chips in cheese and salsa.'
   Crisps

'Keep dry, out of sunlight and chemicals.'
Instant noodles

'Instructions: Put on food.'
Ketchup

'Not meant as substitute for human companionship.'
Throat lozenges

'Why not try tossing over your favourite breakfast cereal?'
Raisin packet

'Made in America. Parts from Japan. Assembled in Mexico'

'All divers must land in water!'
Diving board

'Warning! Improper packing of this parachute may result in serious injury or death to the user!'
Parachute

'Made in America. Parts from Japan. Assembled in Mexico.'
Fender guitar

'This is NOT a life-saving device!'
Life-saving device

'Not recommended for use as a nutcracker.'
Handgun

'Objects are smaller and less alarming than they appear.'
Microscope

'Capacity, 1.'
Wet suit

'Laughs while you throw up'

'Keep out of children.'
Korean kitchen knife

'Warning: Children can drown in bucket, do not place kids in juice.'
Giant bucket of pickles in fast food restaurants

'Keep away from children.'
Baby lotion

'Do not throw baby out with bath water.'
Infant's bathtub

'Remove child before folding.'
Warning on child's stroller pram

'Some assembly required.'
500-piece puzzle

'Let's decompose and enjoy assembling!'
Instructions for a puzzle toy, Taiwan

'Laughs while you throw up.'
Toy doll's package, Spain

'Letters may be used to construct words, phrases and sentences that may be deemed offensive.'
On children's alphabet blocks

'This broom does not actually fly.'
Harry Potter broom

'Wearing of this garment does not enable you to fly.'
On a child's superman costume

'Do not return used condoms to the manufacturer through the mail'

'Take one - two teaspoons full by mouth.'
Cough medicine

'Do not drive a car or run machinery.'
Children's cough medicine

'Do not take if allergic to aspirin.'
Aspirin

'Adults: 1 tablet 3 times a day until passing away.'
Japanese medicine bottle

'Do not use if you are pregnant, intend to become pregnant, or might be pregnant.'
Birth control pills

'Warning: May cause drowsiness.'
Sleep aid

'Caution: Never aim spray at your own eyes.'
Pepper spray

'Do not return used condoms to the manufacturer through the mail.'
Condoms

'WARNING: Do not smoke until hair is dry.'
Hairspray

'Intentional misuse by deliberately concentrating and inhaling the contents can be harmful or fatal.'
Hairspray

'Fits one head.'
Hotel-provided shower cap

'Do not use this product during an earthquake.'
Disposable razor

'CAUTION: This is not a toy.'
Moisture rich body lotion

'Warning: Starts healing skin on contact.'
Bottle of hand lotion

'CAUTION: Avoid contact with face, eyes, and broken skin.'
Peppermint foot spray

'For adult external use only. Avoid spraying in face or eyes.'
Linen spray

'Final step: Pull up underwear.'
Tampons

'Caution: Do not use near power lines'

'Safe to use in households with pets. NOT intended to be sprayed directly on pets.'
> *Fabric spray*

'Start with clean bathtub before use.'
> *Bathtub cleaner*

'Safe for carpets, too!'
> *Carpet cleaner*

'CAUTION: Contains cleaning agents. Do not treat garment while wearing.'
> *Clothes gel*

'Safe to use around pets and children, although it is not recommended that either be permitted to drink from toilet.'
> *Toilet bowl freshener*

'Caution: Do not use near power lines.'
   Toilet plunger

'Directions: Use like regular soap.'
   Hand soap

'Avoid getting in eyes.'
   Shampoo

'May contain foam.'
   Foaming face wash

'Use repeatedly for severe damage.'
   Taiwanese shampoo

'For external use only.'
   Bath treatment

'Not to be used for breast augmentation'

'For best results, do not leave at crime scene.'
Work gloves

'Caution: this tool will cut.'
Machete

'Do NOT swallow nails! May cause irritation!'
Box of household nails

'Do not spray in your face.'
Can of spray paint

'Not to be used for breast augmentation.'
Aerosol for punctured tyres

'Warning: Do not attempt to remove blade while lawnmower is running or plugged into an outlet.'
Push mower

'Do not attempt to stop chain with your hands or genitals.'

Chainsaw, Sweden

'This product not intended for use as a dental drill.'

Powerdrill

'Warning: Do not put any person in this washer.'

Sign on industrial sized washer

'Seat must be facing forward for take off and landing'

'Warning: Do not drive with sunshade in place. Remove from windshield before starting ignition.'
Windshield visor

'Before installing this fan belt, be sure you shut off the engine as it may cause irreversible injury.'
Car fan belt

'Warning: Remove tape before using car seat.'
Car seat with instructional video

'Press this switch to turn on the fart control.'
Car demonstration, Sweden

'Not for highway use.'
Golf cart notice

'Warning: Do not operate vehicle on road, a collision may occur with another vehicle.'
4 x 4 All terrain vehicle

'Avoid Collision.'
On back of barge, Portsmouth Naval Shipyard

'Seat must be facing forward for take off and landing.'
On the back of the pilot's seat on AWAC Aircraft

'Remember, objects in the mirror are actually behind you.'
Helmet mounted mirror used by US cyclists

'Not to be used as protection from a tornado'

'Warning: Do not ignite in face.'
   Lighter

'Do not use near fire, flame, or sparks.'
   Butane lighter

'Caution: Contents may catch fire.'
   Matches

'WARNING: Contents flammable!'
   On container of lighter fluid

'Caution: Risk of fire.'
   Fire logs

'Caution: non-flammable.'
   Fire extinguisher

'Suitable for outdoor use.'
   Rain gauge

'Safe to use around pets.'
  Cat litter

'Shower of Happiness. Total Safety Guaranteed.'
  Label on electric shower, Thailand

'This product not tested on animals.'
  New Zealand insect spray

'Not to be used as protection from a tornado.'
  Blanket from Taiwan

'Do not cut up and use for blackmail note.'
  The Washington Post

'Nothing sucks like an Electrolux!'

'Horse manure 50p per pre-packed bag,
20p do-it-yourself.'
   Outside a farm

'For sale: an antique desk suitable for lady with thick legs
and large drawers.'
   Classified ad.

'For sale: a quilted high chair that can be made into a
table, potty chair, rocking horse, refrigerator, spring coat,
size 8 and fur collar.'
   Classified ad.

'Now is your chance to have your ears pierced and get an
extra pair to take home, too.'

'No matter what your topcoat is made of, this miracle
spray will make it really repellent.'

'For Sale. Three canaries of undermined sex.'
   Classified ad.

'For Sale -- Eight puppies German Shepherd and an Alaskan Hussy.'
   Classified ad.

'Great Dames for sale.'
   Advert in shop window

'Lost: small apricot poodle. Reward. Neutered. Like one of the family.'
   Advert in shop window

'Home wanted for friendly Labrador. Will eat anything - loves children.'
   Advert in shop window

'Tired of cleaning yourself? Let me do it.'
   Advert in shop window

'Vacation Special: have your home exterminated.'
   Advert in shop window

'Get rid of aunts: Zap does the job in 24 hours.'

'Stock up and save. Limit: one.'

'For Rent: 6-room hated apartment.'
   Classified ad.

'Very cultural polish family (she's an electronic, he's a carpenter) is looking for a flat.'
   Classified ad.

'Man, honest. Will take anything.'
Classified ad.

'Shop assistant required. No objection to sex.'
Supermarket notice

'Smart young man for butcher's. Able to cut, skewer and serve customers.'
Advert

'Wanted: chambermaid in rectory. Love in, $200 a month. References required.'

'Man wanted to work in dynamite factory. Must be willing to travel.'

'3-year-old teacher needed for pre-school. Experience preferred.'

'Illiterate? Write today for free help.'

'Mother's helper--peasant working conditions.'

'And now, the Superstore--unequaled in size, unmatched in variety, unrivaled inconvenience.'

'Nothing sucks like an Electrolux!'
Swedish company advert in USA

'For sale, 4-poster bed, 101 years old. Perfect for an antique lover.'

'My recreations are different: travelling, reading, gardening, hooking'

Nice, lonely, modest woman

(45/170/85, economist) with a sense of humour, is looking for a kind, educated Norwegian man for correspondence and maybe marriage.

My recreations are different: travelling, reading, gardeing, hooking, sewing and so on. I don't like the lonely life.

Please send me your photo and describe yourself. write to me in English, please (I know Norwegian language very little).

Nice woman

To a man

I am a 19 y.o. Russian Girl, 168/60. I am a graduate from college. My interests: Heading, Booking, homelife, music, knitring, and I am fond of skiing.

I would like to meet a man without bad habits for friendship or more, a man who is king, trustworthy and intelligent.

Lena

Norwegian girls, look here!

I am a young man from Ghana, age 19, with a sincere interest for Norway and Norwegian girls. I want to exchange letters with girls from your country. I hope this will lead to friendship, or hopefully marriage with a beautiful Norwegian girl.

I always dream about Norway and its beautiful nature. My dream is to build a future life together with a charming Norwegian girl, from age 18 and upwards.

I am dark in complexion, my eyes are light red, and I have a bushy hair, and I am about 2 metres tall. In my leisure time I like to listen to music, play football and read, f.ex. magazines.

I look very much forward to your letter.

Norway in my heart

---

friends with a kind and reliable Norwegian man who does more than speak.

My likes: travels, Booking pizza.

My dislikes: people who speak a lot about nothing.

Write in English, please.

Julija

'Teacher, widower, seeks to meet widow for fiendship.'
Local paper, England